Jan,
Hope you
get a kick
out of these
fun tales!

xo
margot
(Rose)

Not So Prim Rose

The misadventures
of Rose Bush,
flower mag
irreverent

D0998857

WRITTEN BY MARGOT SHAW

ILLUSTRATED BY CLAIRE CORMANY

First Printing 2011
Published by Peony Publishing LLC

Ordering information: Special quantity
discounts are available. For details, contact
the publisher at www.flowermag.com

Rose Bush tackles a daunting task in:

nightmare at the museum

AS MANY OF YOU KNOW, Birmingham is a veritable "hot bed" of flowering folks—male and female. Historically, I have not been among them. But about four years ago I fell head over heels in love with flowering and have not wavered in my affections since.

Imagine my shock and awe when I got the call to participate in "Art in Bloom"—the biannual Birmingham Museum of Art event where flower artists interpret works of art in the museum collection and/or, in the case of 2006, several Comme des Garçons dresses (generously loaned by the patroness de tout patronesses, Carolyn Wade).

The list of participants is long. The list of women involved in bringing this into being is longer. The list of reasons I felt utterly inadequate, longer still.

However, after brief chats with my husband, my cousin (a flower diva in her own right), and the man upstairs, I was in. Then I went to the orientation meeting. I was in alright, in over my head.

The slides we were shown of past participants' pieces were glorious, brilliant, clever, exquisite, creative—in other words, totally intimidating. As I trembled in the dark of the auditorium, my cousin, the diva, patted my hand and said casually, "You'll be fine." Hmmm…

I learned that I was to depict Corot's "Nymphes et Faunes."

I had some ideas. Mainly, I knew I wanted to use a mirror to represent the stream in this lovely landscape, and I wanted somehow to have Debussy's "Afternoon of a Faun" playing alongside my flowers.

From conception to birth was a whole 'nother column. Suffice it to say that I had to do something universally repugnant—I had to ask for help—every step of the way, from my husband, a MacGyver type whose motto is, "Don't spend money on that; I can make one," to the adolescent computer nerd genius guy at the iPod store.

But it got done. And it all worked. Sort of.

A good friend helped me assemble the assemblage the day of the installation. (I could never have wrapped that vine around my iPod cord like she did—my hands were shaking too badly.)

When all was done, we packed up and cleaned up, and went about the all-important task of snooping around to see what everyone else was up to. I was dazzled, and stimulated. All that creativity swirling around in one building was downright energizing.

My husband and I returned that night for the Preview Party.

Party I did not. I was too preoccupied with whether people were able to make the iPod work on my "work."

Apparently they succeeded, as did many others throughout the exhibit. By Saturday morning (two days after the Preview Party) the battery was dead, and the leaf camouflaging the iPod was singed and smelly. (Note to self: Bring adolescent computer nerd genius guy from iPod store next time.)

I did receive numerous bon mots and pats on the back from the flower "powers that be"—and all in all felt honored, humbled, and somewhat bemused that a girl, who never put jonquils in a jelly jar before 2003, had a piece in a gallery next to a Camille Corot. ❧

Rowdy groomsmen topple
Rose Bush's topiaries in:

french fried

ONCE, IN AN APARTMENT far, far away—
Lausanne, Switzerland, to be precise—I was
introduced to Francophilia, believe it or not.
My father, who moved us there for business
reasons, was determined that, since we were
a stone's throw away from the great source

of so many things wonderful and beautiful (i.e., France), we would be exposed to and educated to appreciate these "things."

It worked. My brother and I, young sponges that we were, picked up French, albeit with a slight sing-songy lilt that is common in the Canton de Vaux. (We would later be mocked and ridiculed mercilessly in our adult travels to France by snooty *garçons*.)

We also picked up a love of art (Winged Victory of Samothrace—much more impressive than that stodgy old Mona Lisa who had been so built up by our parents), music (Sylvie Vartan, Françoise Hardy, and Johnny Hallyday), and of course the ubiquitous gourmet fare. Though I much preferred the tartine et chocolat to the trout meunière, and still do.

When we returned to our native Alabama a few years after we'd left, my mother, in an attempt to replicate our Swiss/French environment, covered my bedroom in blue toile and forced me to speak French to her, even in front of my friends—which was utterly degrading and humiliating for a nine-year-old. They all thought I was a terrible show-off.

Though having experienced a few French traumas, I found myself drawn to the language, customs, and style throughout high school, college, and the rest. So, it seemed natural when asked to do the flowers and décor for my goddaughter's nuptials that I should cull from the aesthetic I was weaned on.

First and foremost, there would be topiaries, numerous topiaries. A vestige of Versailles was the feel I was going for. After diligent searching via phone and visits to area nurseries, I came up with seven. Clearly, I would have to explore other allées. I called my landscaper, a can-do guy if I ever met one.

"Sure, no sweat. How many you need?" was his reply.

I had calculated that in order to turn the wedding reception into the vision of Versailles I longed for, I'd need at least 50 large topiaries. Single-ball and double-ball junipers, gardenias, and yellow-gold lantanas. Perfect. I knew I could sell them once the wedding was over.

All went well with the design. I planned to recapitulate the round forms in all the floral arrangements using shades of merlot, marigold, hot green, yellow, and apricot. I also recapitulated the round forms, somewhat, in pluots, nectarines, and lemons carefully mounded at each topiary's base. A lovely French flourish à la Christian Tortu.

That is, until the young groomsmen and their friends, after a few glasses of champagne

(French, of course), began eyeing the fruit with mischievous intent.

The next thing I knew, fruit fights to rival "Animal House" and much juggling ensued. (Someone later asked the mother of the bride if she paid extra for the jugglers.) I even heard that a neighborhood pooch found great relief on one of the outside topiaries. All-purpose topes.

The wedding was a huge success, and a good time was had by all. But meanwhile, if anyone should like to purchase a topiary at a greatly reduced price, please contact me through the *flower* website.

My house and garden are looking decidedly French, which I would love, ordinarily, but it's a shingle, Dutch farm house. ❧

flower magazine launches in Atlanta, despite a freak accident on I-85 in:

almost gone with the wind

WOE BE UNTO YOU when you think you have all your peonies in place.

I had dotted every *i* and crossed every *t* concerning the March 21st *flower* magazine launch party at the Atlanta Botanical Garden. I was feeling pretty confident when, around lunchtime, I arrived to survey the space and heard those words that, though meant to comfort, strike fear and dread into the heart of a hostess/wife: "Your husband called, and he's fine, but there's been a little accident."

Many of you may recall my MacGyver-like husband from the first "Not So Prim Rose" column. Well, in this scenario his talents were put to use bringing 10 wooden pedestals to Atlanta from Birmingham in a recycled rental trailer that had definitely seen better days.

He was almost home free when, as he tells it, he had exited I-20 onto I-85, around the curving ramp, and was sailing into Atlanta. He heard a loud crash, looked in the rearview mirror, and scarily, saw nothing. Then, all at once, he witnessed sparks flying, cars swerving, the detached trailer careening through lanes of traffic, landing on the other shoulder, wobbling, and coming to a stand still. All the while, my MacGyver focused on slowing down, praying hard, helpless to affect the outcome.

Miraculously, not one car or truck was struck by the projectile trailer. But that still left the problem of how to get the pedestals to the party. Our intrepid purveyor simply pulled onto the shoulder of the exit and proceeded to reverse to the point of ejection. He then jumped out of his truck and began to portage the pedestals one by one from the trailer (which at this point was smoking and minus one wheel) into his truck. Six fit in the back, and the last four were strapped to the roof in true MacGyver fashion with a bungee cord and a few dog leashes. At which point, he slowly proceeded to the venue, where he was met by me and all the floral designs that were waiting to perch on the plinths.

Hours later after a hot shower and much head shaking and recounting of the incident, we arrived at the garden and proceeded to enjoy a splendid launch party, complete with sumptuous food, marvelous company, and exquisite flowers.

I think it was all the sweeter in view of the averted disaster. This *flower* business is an adventure, to say the least, and I wouldn't have it any other way. Next stop—Nashville, where we used indigenous pedestals. ❧

An Easter weekend wedding party
feels more like Christmas in:

bad friday

AS I PEN THIS PIECE, I will be preparing to
attend a wedding in the mountains of North
Carolina. Ahhh, relief from Alabama's pun-
ishing Indian summer. Though I look forward
to the cool breezes of October in the Smokies,
a mere five months ago I would have welcomed the swelter.

{ NOT SO PRIM ROSE }

My husband and I and 12 other couples gave an engagement party at our house, to celebrate the upcoming mountain nuptials. We thought Friday, April 6th, would be the perfect date, as many would be home for Easter that weekend, and the weather would most likely be temperate. We were half right.

The theme for the evening was rustic and informal—mountain mojitos in Mason jars, dining tables sporting burlap tablecloths, "field" flowers lovingly arranged in larger Mason jars on each table, hurricane lamps, even a trio of bluegrass-y musicians, the "Ishkooda Ramblers"—all to be set up on the lawn.

Throughout the week leading up to the event, I'd been hearing gentle caveats from co-hostesses that a cold snap was in the forecast. Each time, I threw my head back and laughed saying, "Those guys are never right!" or "Yeah? Well, that's why they make blue jean jackets."

I did concede to allow the hostesses to deliver two fire pits. *I'll humor 'em,* I thought to myself.

Fast forward to the afternoon of the party: lovely, sunny, a little breezy. Tables, cloths, flowers, jars, and lanterns were all delivered. We began to set up.

My first indication that I had perhaps misjudged the accuracy of the forecast came when the Mason jars full of flowers and water kept tumping over. My wonderful, practical sister-in-law suggested putting glass rocks in the bottoms of the jars. We poured every glass rock we could purchase from a nearby floral retailer into the jars and then stood back to admire our genius. Immediately a strong gust knocked EVERY jar over again.

Hmmm. I won't quote the expletives that were hurled, but suffice it to say, we were miffed. The only other solution was to remove the flowers until party time—which we did.

Party time arrived and my husband came in the kitchen to ask if I'd like him to light a fire.

"Why would we need a fire, when it's not cold!?" I snapped. As he walked away, I could hear him murmuring under his breath something about my being in weather denial.

I then peered through the french doors—now closed up tight—and witnessed with a sigh, the first group of guests approaching in jackets, sweaters, pashminas, under down vests, even a hooded ski jacket. And it was only going to get colder as the sun went down.

Now, I'm as game as the next gal, but we were expecting 130, and our house, although quaint and just right for us, holds about 75, and that's pushing it.

Things started out okay, with lots of young people outside listening to the Ramblers. I noticed right away, however, the majority of them huddled around the fire pits.

These kids are lightweights, I observed to myself. I'll start a movement with some of the older, heartier men-folk. A few faithful friends complied, but once I turned my back, they were right back inside, in front of the fire, drinking multiple mountain mojitos.

By mid-party, there was not one square inch of space to be had in the house. Even the Ramblers gave up and came in from the cold. But somehow, no one cared. I looked around and realized the closeness had created a sort of playful, silly atmosphere that allowed (forced) people to engage with whoever was next to them. It was wall-to-wall people, wall-to-wall gaiety, late into the night—a huge, serendipitous success.

My only regret was, of course, that the flowers got such short shrift. ⚘

Labels on signpost:
Ici
Laba
Plus loin
C'est jusque là
Bonnieux
Au prés de ma blonde
McDonald's
Marseilles
Vous est perdu
Station de service avec des fleurs

A directionally challenged Rose Bush
roams the French countryside in:

la vie en
not so
prim rose

I HAD A whole different "Rose" planned, and
then I went to Provence. One of my all-time
favorite books about France is Peter Mayle's
A Year in Provence. I remember my husband
having a scare years ago, as he came down to

the beach and saw me from behind, my head thrown back, shoulders jerking up and down—he was sure I was having some kind of seizure. In reality I was seized with paroxysms of laughter, as I read Peter's account of les gens du Luberon. I couldn't wait!

My "Tour de France" began with a mapquest from Marseille to Bonnieux. First of all, let me recommend not doing that—mainly because the Marseille airport is not *in* Marseille. I ended up going an hour and a half in the wrong direction to get to the first instruction on mapquest, during which time I stopped in traffic and asked a garbageman directions. Though I am semi-fluent in French, the only word I understood was "McDonald's."

Now, there's a uniquely European way of driving that, though initially unnerving in its seemingly utter disregard for other cars, strangely, kind of works. It took me a few heart-stopping near misses to surrender to the organized chaos of this dance. Once I calmed down enough to proceed, it became abundantly clear that the tangle of signs which appeared at random intervals were no help. There was not a street sign to be found among 'em. I began to pray.

Next, I spotted a random sign that mentioned something familiar: Aix en Provence. I remembered that Bonnieux was in that general direction, so I went "that a way."

Finally out of Marseille, I breathed a sigh of relief. *I'm on my way now.* But as my late father-in-law was fond of saying, "There's many a slip between the cup and the lip."

Though the natives know their land very well, and know exactly what they mean by *la coline la-bas, en droite, vers le bâtiment brun* (the hill over there, on the right, near the brown building), there are lots of hills over there on the right, and plenty of brown buildings. I venture to say that between my initial discovery of the road to Aix and arriving at my destination, I must have gone down eight to 10 wrong roads and stopped almost as many times to ask directions. At one point, I was sure there was a plot perpetrated by locals to keep tourists from finding their way.

Just when I was close to camping out in my rental Renault on the side of the road, I spied a *station de service.* With the cynicism of a weary and beleaguered traveler, I turned in, thinking, *What the heck, I'll give it one more shot*—when what should I spy by the entrance of the station but a huge display of FLOWERS!!!—all kinds, all colors, all shapes, all wrapped in the white butcher paper of the street vendor, all saying, "It's ok, don't worry, we're here, you know us, you're on the right track."

As I asked yet again for directions, I heard those words I'd been longing to hear: *"C'est juste la-bas, un tourne et voilà."* (It's just over there, one turn and you're there.) And it was and I am. ✺

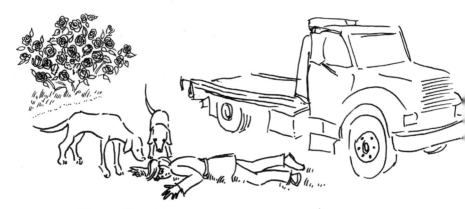

Rose Bush's treacherous trip home starts
with a bang and ends with a fall in:

a hunting I did go and barely did make it back

"HONEY, I CAN'T POSSIBLY go to Mississippi in mid-December for two days on a
hunting trip. A) It's mid-Christmas season
and all that that implies. B) I've got flowerin'
to do. C) I don't hunt."

But I did go, and it was sublime.

We weren't holed up in a cabin with no
amenities in the middle of nowhere. We were
wined, dined, and generally spoiled rotten
in an antebellum home-cum-hunting club,

in the middle of nowhere. Midway through the two days, I began to think maybe I could get used to *this* kind of hunting. I was even looking through Orvis catalogues on the sly before breakfast.

Though I had brought lots of flowerin' work along, I didn't really think I'd have much time to devote. But somehow, I managed to complete two projects and still go along for the ride on a morning hunt. As we were pulling out of the driveway to return home, I smiled at my husband and told him that it had been a perfect trip. He concurred, and we rode along in the afterglow of a successful expedition.

Just outside of Eutaw, Alabama, however, smoke began to shroud our SUV, lights started flashing, and my beloved whipped off the highway and quickly cut the engine. I looked at the dash and EVERY graphic was lit up, including one I'd never seen, of a car with all the doors open—which said to me: "GET OUT! GET OUT NOW!"

So we did.

But once the car was off, the smoke died down. We got back in and called a towing company—an hour and a half away. While we waited, I worked and the great sportsman next to me slept.

Finally, after dark, a huge truck pulled up to

save the day and drove our vehicle up onto the bed, dog box on the back and all. (I kept asking if the dogs could ride in the cab with us, to no avail.)

But we made good time and enjoyed visiting with our tow-truck driver, Johnnie, hearing all about what his nine-year-old little girl wanted for Christmas, and talking about football and the like.

We were all smiles and conviviality as we approached the last mile of our trip, when the truck began coughing and sputtering.

I didn't say a word. I just sat and watched as the unthinkable happened: The tow truck ran out of gas. There in four-lane traffic by the biggest mall in Birmingham (a week before Christmas), we sat shaking our heads.

Johnnie called his office, and they sent help in the form of a little bitty tow truck and a rope—and three guys who reminded me of nothing so much as Larry, Darryl, and his other brother Darryl. Their plan was to use the rope to tow the big truck with the SUV and dog box on it up to the gas station. We had other ideas and talked them into actually going to said station and purchasing gas and coming back with it.

Once we were on our way again, we all laughed and lowed as how this would be one for the books (or magazine in my case). Johnnie took us home before dropping our truck at the shop, for which we were most grateful.

After he backed up our driveway to expedite unloading the dogs and luggage, I thanked him, wished him a Merry Christmas, opened the door of the truck, and—forgetting that I was higher off the ground than usual—fell five feet to the ground, rolled a few feet, and lay there facedown thinking, *I am NEVER going ANYWHERE with my husband again!*

But suddenly, as I realized I was lying on the soft, welcoming carpet of zoisia, I burst out laughing and thought to myself, *Well, I could have landed in the rose garden.*

Rose Bush attends a wedding
for better and worse in:

wedding bell blues

ONE OF MY MANY CHALLENGES in life is
punctuality. I think one reason I'm perpetually
five or 10 minutes late to everything is that
everything always takes longer than I think it
will. This truth was driven home to me in my
days as a flower-shop girl. We would plan the
day's work schedule for a wedding, say, and

allot one hour to put up sprays on sconces at the reception, and sure enough, forget the wire and have to drive back to the shop. Presto! One hour, transformed into three.

So, in preparing to attend the first wedding of spring in my burg, I was determined to "get me to the church on time." To be sure, I checked my laptop calendar: wedding at six at a downtown cathedral.

My daughter and I arrived at 5:15, deliriously happy to have a parking place right by the church and patting ourselves on the back about the great seats we were sure to secure. We leisurely crossed the street and greeted a bridesmaid, seven or eight groomsmen, and the mother of the bride—none of whom seemed overly impressed at our early arrival. As we walked up the steps and into the church, I had a sinking feeling. *Wait a minute, this is too good to be true.*

The church was full of people—none of whom looked dressed for a six o'clock wedding. Furthermore, there was a service in progress. I thought to myself, *Well, they better hurry up in there if this wedding's going to start on time.*

Heading back outside, I stage-whispered to the bridesmaid, "You know there's a service going on? Wait a minute. What time is the wedding?!"

She sheepishly held up seven fingers. I could feel my face flush as my daughter and I had to run the gamut of wedding people back to our car. We went all the way home and came back an hour later.

Surprise! Not a parking place in sight. By the time we got inside, the only seats available were smack-dab behind a massive column. Though a lovely and no doubt structurally necessary architectural detail, it obscured the entire ceremony from our view.

As the recessional played, the heavens opened up. Most days in drought-ridden Birmingham I would welcome the sound of thunder. Not this day.

Sporting silk and no umbrella, I cringed at the sight of everyone else's bumbershoots opening up and the thought of my car, five city blocks away. I looked at my daughter, in her new daffodil-yellow dress with her hair and makeup perfect, and made a snap decision to let her wait against the side of the building under the eaves, while I ran, sploshing through puddles, to fetch the car.

We arrived at the reception just as the deluge ceased and agreed to split up so I could check out the flowers and she could find her friends. I smiled the proud mama smile as I watched her walk away, until I noticed a huge black swath of soot across the lower portion of her new daffodil-yellow dress. I lunged for her and asked her come to the powder room with me. (Only a mom can rub your backside with a wet cloth in the powder room in front of a bunch of strangers from Mississippi.)

Out in the world of the reception, I made my way through a wonderland of sumptuous flowers, jazzy music, and really fun wedding guests. I did not, however, make it to the food. On my way out, I spied a basket full of tulle-wrapped treats and grabbed one. Heading home, I unwrapped the bundle, tossed a Jordan almond into my mouth, and promptly cracked a filling.

I was just recovering from what I hoped was the last challenge of the evening when, walking in my front door and catching my reflection in the mirror, I had yet another jarring moment. Having been so consumed with "getting out damned spot" on my daughter's dress, I neglected to check my own look and had apparently spent the entire reception with rain-flattened hair and streaky makeup.

As I winced at the thought, I looked down, and crumpled in my hand was the card from the candy: "Five Jordan almonds for guests to eat, to remind us that life is both bitter and sweet."

Uh-huhhh... ⭐

Rose Bush's husband MacGyver
is dressed to impress in:

black tie,
white tie,
no tie, oh my!

AS YOU MIGHT IMAGINE, being a *flower* editor, I attend a lot of flowery events. Some could best be described as "snazzy." I bend every effort to look my best, not draw any negative attention to myself, and generally come off as fairly *comme il faut*—and in the process catch up with the event photographer, planner, and floral designer, all the while assessing the floral component for reportage.

Generally, I attend these soirées alone, but lately I've been accompanied by my husband. (Many of you recall his MacGyver–ish adventures from earlier columns.) This addition has proved salutary, as he is remarkable on his feet, cuts quite a dash, and is able to lift heavy objects, such as my suitcases.

The last few events, however, have been marred (for me) by my inability to designate the proper attire for my "date."

First, we traveled out of state to a ball, which I assumed, like many balls, was black tie. We waltzed through the entrance and made our way into the loggia of the old manse, and I immediately broke out into a cold sweat. Every gentleman there was sporting a decidedly non-black tie, i.e., white tie and tails. MacGyver didn't even notice. (Typical male—in a good way.)

Though I had charming dinner partners and was among the first to rush the stage when the talent came on, I spent the evening, by and large, feeling self-conscious for my husband—and by association, me. (I know;

it's awful, but there it is.)

The second sartorial sabotaging occurred when we were set to attend a midsummer wedding in Alabama. It was a six o'clock wedding, which to me says black tie, right? My sweet husband this time had checked with a friend and fellow wedding guest he happened to run into the day of the wedding. "Eastlake says he's not wearing black tie. He doesn't think anyone is," my beloved informed me.

But I insisted on black tie and off we went. We parked and I looked in the side-mirror, and my heart sank as I watched waves of male guests make their way up the church steps in suits, coat and tie, and even NO TIE!

I gave my lips a swipe of lipstick and said to my laughing, yet at this point somewhat chagrined husband, "You may be the only one in black tie, but you're right!"

Scant comfort it was. Another dread-filled entrance ensued as we strolled into the church in which all the men were non-formally attired. I wish I could say that I sat in reverent contemplation waiting for the ceremony to begin, but I'd be lying. I sat, distracted and self/husband-conscious. And this continued throughout the festivities.

I remember that the flowers at both events were fabulous, but don't ask me to be specific.

I'll have to wait for the photographers' discs.

Meanwhile, my MacGyver's next adventure is to wrest all invitations away from me so that *he* can decide what tie to wear. ❧

Rose Bush narrowly escapes
a demonstration disaster in:

midnight at the oasis

"I'M TOO OLD FOR THIS," I groused to my husband on the phone, tucked into my hotel room for the night.

After having driven eight hours and schlepped buckets of flowers and greenery, a toolbox, bags of green Oasis floral-foam spheres, magazine posters, easels, and suitcases along with me, I was duly pooped when

I arrived in a new town earlier that night for a floral convention the next day.

However, I had been quickly revived as I witnessed a police car, siren blaring, blue lights flashing, wheeling into the porte-cochère. As the cruiser sped down the lot in pursuit of the alleged perpetrator, I emerged from my car and proceeded to the check-in counter.

I asked the receptionist what was up, and he casually replied that someone had just been held up at gunpoint in the back parking lot. He then shared that this had never happened before. (What about that statement was supposed to be comforting?) I knew I should've brought my husband, or at least my pepper spray. All I was packing in the way of self-defense were some prickly grasses and a really big pocketbook.

It took two trips to get all the items out of my car, and in view of the proximity of the crime scene, I made haste. I never stopped to ask any details about the convention, just checked in and went straight to my room. After an hour of unloading all my worldly goods into the room and telephoning my husband to regale him with the events of the evening, I began to map out my presentation, scheduled for first thing the next morning.

My plan was to use plant material that was all locally grown or organic (or both) and recycled containers for my demonstration.

Having scored several bunches of sunflowers, I decided to be really modern and edgy and pull all their petals off, stick the eyes in Oasis spheres, and then place them atop big mercury-glass containers.

Without extra buckets, I had to soak the Oasis in my bathtub. I was just putting the last globe in the tub and squinching fountain grass, okra, and other "green" greenery onto the counter when a convention representative called, reminding me of the welcome reception. Okay...

I've shared bathrooms with roommates (many), children (three), and husbands (two), but I've never had to compete for the mirror with poke salad.

After a quick turn around the party, I raced back up to my room-cum-flower shop. I still had my sunflower spheres to do and lots of dividing of grasses and flowers. Grabbing my snips, I began to behead the sunflowers and de-petal them. All were neatly laid out on a towel in my room as I lifted the first Oasis sphere out of the tub (which, of course, by this time was filled with green water and multiple bobbing balls).

I began poking the short stems into the Oasis, and just as I would poke the next one in, the one before would fall out. (Note to self: Always do a dry run before a demo/presentation.)

So, I had now cut the heads off several bunches of organic sunflowers and soaked numerous Oasis balls, only to be able to use neither. The only other flowers I could have used were zinnias, but their stems are too soft. Lacking any picks, I decided to punt the whole cool-globe concept.

This meant I was effectively done for the evening, as the remaining plant material was all to be used in my demo the following day.

Bright and early the next morning, I began to run my shower, only to realize I had to dispose of the soaked, now 10-pound Oasis balls. Ughhh. So I picked up the phone and bellowed, "HOUSEKEEPING!!!!!"

This was turning into a real logistical night-mare. After getting dressed and loading all my flowers back onto a luggage cart, I wheeled down to the lobby to locate the venue for my presentation. A half-mile later inside the convention center, I found my space. I steered straight for it and started to turn in, when what should I spy directly across the hall but a HUGE flower-filled room equipped with tables, buckets, sinks—you get the picture—and all the other presenters working on their designs.

I may have missed this particular piece of information in my haste the night before, but I did manage to avoid the night bandit, pull together a presentation, and determine to use the buddy system for future travels. ❧

A trip to New York turns a little too hip in:

heartbreak hotel

WHILE STEPPING OUT OF THE CAB from the airport one evening in New York City, and looking forward to the sanctuary of the posh hotel before me, my dreams were dashed by techno music blaring from hidden speakers— meant, I'm sure, to impart a cool, sophisticated vibe to arriving guests. But to me, a travel-weary, middle-aged *flower* gal, it imparted, "What are *you* doing here? This place is for scenesters and celebrities!"

As I tried desperately to identify the doorman from among a scrum of black-clad street dudes, the cab driver took pity on me and signaled one of said dudes to help with my bags. (How he was able to pick out the hotel employee is beyond me.) I thanked him with the first bill I could find in my wallet and proceeded warily and shakily into a lobby that reminded me of the bar scene in the first "Star Wars" movie.

Next challenge: to locate/identify the registration desk. Though there were several really sleek, modern surfaces in this area, all with polished chrome bowls filled with polished Granny Smith apples, not a one of them possessed the requisite polished person to check me in.

As I stood in this vortex of futuristic isolation, I prayed quietly for help, *I need somebody*, then crazily giggled to myself imagining the Lennon/McCartney scenario that prompted those lyrics. On the heels of this sacred moment, a gentleman appeared behind one of the sleek surfaces, staring at me in mild amusement. "Welcome to the hotel. Checking in?"

After successfully accomplishing that mission, I endeavored to locate the elevators. They, like everything else, were discreet and (to these eyes) unrecognizable. I stood and waited for other guests who looked like they might be "going up" and promptly followed them as the cave-like Aladdin's doors opened. Aha! They used their room key to get to their floor, but strangely, after they disembarked, my key did not grant the magical access I was by this time SO longing for.

Struggling to tune out the ubiquitous techno strains and figure out the secret motion that would get me to the Valhalla of my room and bed, I found myself grumbling to myself, as I had on several other *flower* escapades, "I'm too old for this."

Finally, after holding my mouth just right and clicking my heels together three times, I was mercifully delivered to my floor, room, and bed. Things were looking up, until I tried in vain to turn off the clock radio. Though tuned to a much more soothing classical station, I still needed—no, craved—silence.

To avoid tearing the clock out of the wall, I did what any middle-aged parent of a 20-something would do in this situation: I telephoned my daughter for technical support. She lovingly helped me navigate the buttons with hardly a chuckle and offered to help me figure out the mini-bar. I responded that I somehow always managed to access the cache of chocolates and nut mixes in the "bar" (unfortunately), but thanked her very much.

The next day, after a good night's sleep, I considered that I might have a smoother time of it in the "brave new world" of my hotel, but I was mistaken. I could not access the fitness room (not due to any technical difficulty, but rather an early-morning, rush-hour mob scene unlike anything I had ever seen). So I returned to my room, busted a few Pilates moves on the paper-thin commercial carpet, showered, dressed, packed, called an old favorite hotel, and booked a room for the rest of my stay.

Sailing out of the space odyssey lodgings, I glimpsed a blur of color in the niches of the bar. Ever the flower fanatic, I turned back—and there, in a perfect twist of irony, sat the most exquisite floral designs I'd seen in a long time. I asked the doorman to hold my cab while I found the nearest polished person and promptly ascertained the name of their florist. ⚘

Rose Bush and the *flower* girls encounter rats, cats, and rascals in:

animal house work

ONLY LOCAL *FLOWER* READERS are aware of the fact that our office is located in my guest house. We call it the "International Headquarters" of *flower* magazine. More humorous when we first launched, we are now actually on newsstands in 18 countries. Meanwhile, we remain in the "IHQ."

Though this affords a great savings in overhead and lends a casual-Friday feel to every day, it has its drawbacks. Ordinarily, these little foxes nibble at the vines only on occasion. Yesterday, the whole vineyard came down.

In my line of work, I travel a good bit, attending and speaking at floral and garden events. One day on my return from the road, I was greeted by my daughter, who had arrived home for a visit. Heading to her room in the guest house (over the IHQ), she promptly fled back downstairs into the office hollering that there was some disgusting smell in her room.

After a collective sigh (and thinking she was a bit of a princess) we *flower* girls strode upstairs to get to the bottom of things. On entering, we were assaulted by the horrible odor of a dead animal—at which point, screaming *flower* girls stampeded back down the stairs.

Our hero, David of Athena Pest Control (named by the owners of the company after the Greek goddess of war, because they realize it's an ongoing battle), had set traps, and one had apparently worked. In response to our call, David arrived on the scene and was given a standing ovation by all *flower* girls present as he very efficiently and somewhat proudly carried out the pest in a garbage bag and, with it, the awful odor.

Back to work we went, sure that the worst of our animal troubles were over. Not so.

Our managing editor, due to the somewhat relaxed environment in the IHQ, had taken to periodically bringing her rescue kitten to work. Usually this was not a problem, and on this particular day, said kitty had been left at home. However, my daughter's kitty had also made the trip home and didn't much care for the scent of the other woman.

We know this, because when we all got back from lunch, we experienced yet another unpleasant animal odor: Visiting kitty had apparently picked up the other feline fragrance from the managing editor's computer bag and proceeded to display her displeasure in that uniquely charming way cats have—she tee-teed all up in that bag.

Lovely.

I mentioned that I'd love to stay and help clean up, but remembered I had to go cover a very important flower show and beat a hasty retreat.

The show was fabulous, and many there had seen the magazine and subscribed. *Maybe this won't be such a bad day after all,* I thought to myself. As I drove back to the IHQ, I reminisced with a warm glow about the past few days of travel, which had consisted of fabulous floral parties and events filled with fun, creative people, amazing flowers and gardens, and warm receptions.

As I exited my car back at the office, I was still thinking along overly confident lines: *Life is good! We're in high cotton now! This is the stuff! Wow, I can't believe how far we've come! How great is this!*

Right then and there, I was suddenly and rather harshly brought down to earth. As I unloaded my accoutrements right in front of the IHQ, with *flower* girls gazing out the window at the scene, my husband's bird dog proceeded to casually lift his leg on my *flower* bag, turn, and lope off after yet another enticing target. He was obviously not as impressed with me or the magazine as I was.

We have been soft-searching for just the right office space for about a year now, but in light of these recent incidents, it looks like we may escalate our efforts. ☀

Rose Bush relates her travel
trials and tribulations in:

ramblin' woes

AS I'VE MENTIONED BEFORE, travel is a
big part of my life as a *flower* editor. Since
9/11, travel in general has become more or
less a case of, "How bad do you want to go?"

Some of my peregrinations pass more or
less without incident—others, no so much.
This account deals with two back-to-back
trips (never a good idea) that went awry.

Unfortunately, I am unable to blame either incident on terrorists.

First, I was headed on Sunday afternoon to New Orleans via Southwest Airlines (one of my favorites due to their democratic seating and the zany, cornball, Southern humor of their pilots and flight attendants). I sat at my gate (or so I thought) and settled in for a 45-minute wait during which I delved into the newest *Vogue*. Suddenly, I realized my flight was really late, but they hadn't made any announcements. And no one at the gate seemed particularly concerned.

I got up and went to the attendant, at which point I learned with horror that I was at the wrong gate and my flight had departed. Of course, there were no more flights to be had that night. So, I did what any *flower* gal who was slated to be on TV at 6 a.m. in NOLA the next day would do—I hopped in my car and drove.

The trip was lovely, and I arrived without incident and slept for a whole three hours. When I got to the station and shared the story of my travel fiasco, the anchor of the morning show just laughed and said, "We could've filled that three minutes, no problem. You should have called."

What!? I'm expendable, replaceable; the

show could have gone on without me!? Apparently. But I went on and pulled together a quick design, spread *flower* magazine love and advice, and left.

With no rest for the weary, the very next morning my trusty assistant and I had to drive to Atlanta for a garden club appearance. Only a two-hour drive, no sweat. NOT.

Evidently, the much-prayed-for rains had finally come to Georgia and flooded the entire area from 40 miles out of Atlanta, through the city, and out the other side. What was usually two hours quickly became five. My trusty (24-year-old) assistant had maps and apps all over her Blackberry and set about finding alternate routes for us.

Sadly, what often happened was we would sneakily take a turn and think, *Aha! We're free at last!,* only to find bumper-to-bumper traffic or road blocks where bridges or roads were washed out and not showing up on her apps and maps.

Meanwhile, T.A. (my trusty assistant) was texting the ladies in the garden club with updates, thinking they would say, "Oh, just turn around and go back; this is too much; you'll be too late." But no. These were garden-loving women who had gathered, cooked, and decorated and were going to wait out the vicissitudes of our travel and even find people to pick up their children at noon—all to hear about *flower* and glean a few design tips. God love 'em.

We finally rolled in as the meeting was set to end, but most members had stayed. As we rushed in with our flowers and containers, the women welcomed us with enthusiasm and gratitude, incredulous that we had arrived. I proceeded to speak and demo with more humor and enthusiasm than ever before, I think, due to the thrill and flush of coming through yet another traveling trial.

We drove back pretty much the way we came (it took exactly another five hours, maps and apps included) and pulled up to the IHQ. We were greeted by staffers wondering what took us so long—to which we responded, "How much time do you have?" ⚘

A car trip without coolant
turns into a hot mess in:

ramblin' woes, part 2

IT MUST SEEM BY NOW to readers that I am the world's worst traveler. It's entirely possible.

When I finished my last installment, I thought I'd have to cast about for a new topic for the next column. *Surely no more "bad trips."* Wrong.

Recently, T.A. (my trusty assistant) and I drove to Huntsville, Alabama, for a *flower* event. We left Birmingham bright and early and were making good time, so I was reluctant to stop when my coolant level light flashed on. I called my husband, who you know as "MacGyver" and asked if I could make it. "Sure, honey. Just stop at a fillin' station after the show and get some coolant."

All went well in the Rocket City, and we got back on the road at a more rapid speed than usual, as T.A. had a bachelorette party in Atlanta to attend. We were flying down I-65 when, all of a sudden, the steering wheel would barely turn, the screen started flashing, and a terrible smell filled the air.

"OH #@$*%!"

Of course, I had neglected to stop and get coolant, and just north of Cullman, Alabama, my car went on strike.

I pulled over slowly into the "V" between the interstate and a merging lane, scared I couldn't make it all the way across the next lane to the shoulder. So, off the road but in the tiniest patch of grass imaginable, with semis, pick-ups, and cars blowin' by us on both sides like we were at the Talladega 500 or something, I got out with my bottle of Dasani and popped the hood. I thought I'd just pour a little water in there and fix 'er right up. Wrong again.

So I called Roadside Assistance (or should I say "Roadside Resistance"). I read the VIN number to the woman on the other end, and she came back with, "I'm sorry, but your car's no longer under warranty." *Okay, I guess I'll just stay here then . . .*

"Well," I responded calmly, "that's okay; I'll pay for the wrecker."

"What is your location?" the voice on the other end said.

I told her, to which she responded, "Are you sure?"

And it deteriorated from there. The last helpful response she gave consisted of, "We can't find a wrecker near Cullman; we'll have to send one from Birmingham. He'll be there in about an hour and a half. Oh, yes, and he doesn't take credit cards or checks, but he said he'd be glad to run you by an ATM machine."

I curtly responded, "Thanks. We'll handle it from here."

T.A and the managing editor, back at the International Headquarters, joined forces. M.E. Googled Cullman wrecker services, T.A.

made the call, and Presto! Fifteen minutes later, up roared Steve, originally from Spearfish, South Dakota, with his wrecker and double cab, a lovely attitude, and "Yes, ma'am, I take American Express."

The next thing I knew, I was snug in the back seat of the wrecker and headed home, my cute little car with the *flower* magazine license plate staring me in the face in the rear window. Thinking I'd escaped unscathed, I found out T.A. had taken a picture with her phone of the car in tow and sent it out with color commentary on Twitter and Facebook.

Ah, the two-edged sword of technology— helped and humiliated all in the span of a half hour. ❧

Rose Bush learns the
importance of research in:

rose of sharon joad

DESPITE THE MANY MISHAPS recorded in
previous stories, I continue to travel and represent *flower* magazine. However, it's one
thing for your car to break down in a small

town and quite another to show your you-know-what in a big city in front of a lot of big-wigs.

The phone call that precipitated my latest comeuppance: "Ms. Bush, we would love for you to speak at our antiques show. The last speaker was Renny Reynolds, and before that, P. Allen Smith."

WHOA.

"What do you think your topic might be?"

Rather than get back to her later, I felt compelled to come with a response: "How 'bout antique roses and roses in antiques?"

"Perfect!" the caller exclaimed.

HELP.

Now, I know a little bit about roses, enough to be dangerous. But having studied art history in college and wintered at Winterthur Museum, I thought, *Well, at least the antique part's in the bag.*

I got started right away and did what any middle-aged dilettante would do; I commissioned an intern to do the research. Every day for weeks the IHQ looked like an "all-nighter" in a college dorm—with books and legal pads and laptops spread hither and yon.

Plus, I called local and regional experts, interviewed the premier rosarian in my neck of the woods, and read all the notes compiled by our intern. I even listened to Sting's version of a medieval Christmas carol, "There is No Rose of Such Virtue," to get into the spirit.

The intern put together a flawless Power-Point comprised of rose history and past *flower* magazine articles on roses, as well as some choice images of well-documented antiques bearing rose motifs. The last component of my presentation was to be a demonstration of the ever-popular French hand-tied bouquet using antique roses, of course. And I had cleverly chosen an antique silver vessel as container for said hand-tied.

The presentation went smoothly. I miraculously kept all the rose facts and names and such straight during the PowerPoint, and I sailed through the roses in antiques part, as well as the demo. I crowned the presentation with a quick reference to the provenance of my antique container, took a bow, and exited the stage, fairly glowing with a mix of self-satisfaction and relief.

Not so fast.

As I began my tour of the antiques show, my first stop was a booth purveying antique silver. I graciously admired the dealer's wares and suddenly spotted the exact same style container that I had used.

"Oh, I see you have the same tea caddy I

used in my demonstration!" I exclaimed.

"Ahem. Actually," the dealer commented, "that's a biscuit box. Several women came in after your presentation and checked with me."

Aaarrrgggghhhhh.

In researching rose terms in preparation for my presentation, I had come across an old familiar character from *The Grapes of Wrath*, Rose of Sharon Joad. The description I read of her? "Full of self-importance and false confidence."

Ouch. ⚘

A long day runs the gamut between
nobility and hairballs in:

royal pains

IN CASE YOU, DEAR READER, are laboring
under the misconception that my life is a bed
of roses—perhaps say, those few who've not
followed my peregrinations and humiliations
in this column—allow me to disabuse you of
that notion as I chronicle a day in the life of
Rose Bush: Monday, June 14th, 2010.

{ NOT SO PRIM ROSE }

I rise at 3 a.m. in order to have coffee and go over my notes in preparation for a 4 a.m. phone interview with a duchess, who lives in the U.K. (I wish you could have seen all the *flower* girls the Friday before, Googling "how to address a duchess" so that I didn't start off with a faux pas.)

The hour-long conversation is delightful, but then I'm too stimulated to go back to sleep. I press on through the morning in a bit of a fog—finding myself lapsing into a slight British accent here and there.

Mid-afternoon, out in the *flower* IHQ (my guest house), it's business as usual until our editorial assistant suddenly swoops over to whisk the printer off the top of a chest of drawers. I look up and realize she's saving it from certain drowning, as we have a leak. No rain, mind you, just a leak, emanating from the ceiling—just behind my desk. Awesome.

I call our air-conditioning contractor (on speed dial for this over-50 gal), and they send over Eugene—Eugene of the dear, meek monotone and sweet countenance, who matter-of-factly informs me that it "doesn't look good." Prepared for the worst, I pull out my checkbook, but Eugene is not through. Next, he asks for a garbage bag so that he can carry out the two rodents he's come across while investigating the leak. (Thank God for men.)

As Eugene attempts his exit, stage left, the big brown truck pulls up and blocks him in. (IT'S THE SUMMER ISSUE!) More chaos ensues as all the *flower* girls try to avoid contact with the garbage bag and move boxes around to make room for more boxes, all the while squealing with a mix of disgust re: the rodents, and glee re: the magazine.

At the end of this long, colorful day, I think, *Well, now I can relax with a hot soak and a good night's sleep.* But apparently not.

First of all, I walk into the house to discover that the bird dog/billy goat has torn up the box containing my new dress for a family wedding, hot off the brown truck with the magazines. *Never mind, I can go shopping in the basement.*

Next? I trudge up to my bathroom to soak and find not one, but two hairballs in my tub courtesy of my cat, Marigold.

So I shower instead.

I tumble into bed next to my husband (whom many of you know as MacGyver, but whom some of you also know as an Episcopal priest) and fall instantly into a deep and well-deserved slumber. A few hours later, I'm well into REM sleep, and the phone rings (on my side of the bed).

It's the alarm company calling to inform us

that someone has broken into my husband's church. I turn on the light and read until he returns two hours later.

As I thrash around, trying in vain to sleep, I notice the time: 4 a.m. *I could call the duchess. I know she's up.* ❧

Hydrangeas take a hit during
a *flower* delivery in:

isn't that special, delivery

ONE OF THE HIGHLIGHTS of working at *flower* is the arrival of the new issue. Generally, this occurs midmorning, when a brown truck pulls up to the International Headquarters and a man with a dolly brings us our precious cargo.

Most recently, however, this was not the case. Interestingly, our managing editor had no sooner prodded me for a new "Not So Prim Rose" than I received a phone call from Derrick the truck driver saying, "Ms. Bush, I've got your magazines. I'm down on the lane, but I'm in an 18-wheeler and can't get up your driveway. Can you come down and get the boxes?"

No, but I can send some young flower *girls with their SUVs.*

The much-anticipated magazine was the fall issue. It was September in Alabama and therefore 97 degrees and humid. Derrick, in his air-conditioned cab, definitely had the better end of this deal.

I went back to work and then promptly received a phone call from my trusty assistant, who said, "You'd better get down here. There's a problem."

As I stomped out the door, I mentioned over my shoulder to our managing editor, "Stay tuned. I think we may have a 'Rose' in the works."

I arrived at the bottom of the driveway to spy the 18-wheeler lodged (actually more like stuck) at an angle across the lane—nose in the middle of my neighbor's driveway across the street. Apparently Derrick was unable to negotiate the Austin Powers 15-point turn that would have extricated him from the wrong driveway. Not only was he stuck, but in the process, he'd trenched my neighbor's yard and pulled down a few hydrangea bushes in the bargain.

But the BEST part was that my neighbor was idling in her driveway, waiting to get out. Not only had she witnessed the carnage, she was now trapped. After profuse apologies and much groveling, I helped Derrick back up, straighten up, and head down the lane so that my neighbor could exit.

That done, we began to unload the boxes and place them in the backs of the SUVs. Let me remind you, it's September in Alabama, and we were all immediately in need of showers and big glasses of iced tea. Next, Derrick attempted to back up the lane to the main street.

"Hold on, I'll guide you," said I, with all the bravado of one who's trying to instill confidence when she is completely out of her depth.

Not in possession of the requisite orange aircraft marshalling batons, I resorted to wild flailing and gesticulating in an effort to direct Derrick backwards to the main road and to freedom.

You know the rest. Every time I got him almost completely backed onto the road, a stream of cars would pull up and need to get past. Derrick, eyes rolling, would inch back down the lane and let them by. This went on for a good while, when finally he was able to fully back out onto the main road and high-tail it. He left without a wave or a goodbye, just a roar of the engine and blue-gray diesel fumes hanging in the air. (Bless his heart. I know he was done.)

I slogged back up to the IHQ with a few choice words in mind for the trucking company, but in possession of what I thought was most likely my next Prim Rose dispatch. As I walked in and relayed the story to our managing editor, she smiled, shrugged, and said, "Well, unfortunately, you cannot say that no flowers were harmed in the delivery of this magazine."

Funny. ⌘

Rose Bush's vacation goes from relaxing to vexing in:

tough break

THOUGH I TRAVEL A LOT for *flower*, I rarely vacate or recreate. I don't usually take notice of this until I find myself repeating myself, misplacing things (i.e. wallet in the freezer, etc.), sitting in front of my laptop unable to recall why, and begging my husband to go to fabulous parties without me—all signs of a much-needed break.

The week between Christmas and New Year's Eve is historically pretty quiet in my *flower* world, so I settled on that time to travel to a country inn north of Birmingham and enjoy time away with my husband. In hindsight, "enjoy" might be too strong a word.

A drive of only a few hours brought us to an idyllic spot that yielded sighs of pleasure—which quickly turned to sighs of exasperation. For starters, the innkeeper had us scheduled to arrive the next day. So the heat was not turned on, and we were experiencing what seemed like the coldest snap in state history, but by morning the icicles began to melt off my nose.

We started to warm up and settle in, and after a day of reading and relaxing, we began to prepare for a semi-swishy soirée at some friends' mountain house nearby. Though I'm not a huge stylista, I do like to come off as at least well groomed.

Plan thwarted.

As I turned on the blow dryer, I heard a crack like gunfire, and the whole room went dark. My husband, aka MacGyver, was unable to remedy the problem, as I had apparently done more damage than just a blown fuse.

(Old houses can be so charming.) Luckily, we were the only guests in the inn, so we had our pick of rooms to move to later on. But meanwhile, I arrived at the party sporting limp, damp, somewhat-frozen hair, and a bit of an attitude.

Our next fun surprise, once moved to our new room, was being awoken at 2 a.m. by a chirping smoke detector. You know the kind. They chirp, then stop, and you think it's over and are just drifting back to sleep when they chirp again.

We called security, and they sent over Otis, who basically helped my husband move a table so that he (my husband) could get on top of it and dismantle the smoke detector. (Thanks, Otis!) As you can imagine, after this adventure, we lay there, wide awake for hours, running the emotional gamut between furious and highly amused.

The last day of our relaxing getaway was relatively uneventful, which was a relief since I woke up with a sore throat, cough, and a fever of 101. At that point, I couldn't wait to get home and rest up from my vacation. ⫯

flower girls encounter serious car-tastrophes in:

blooms off the roads

ONE THING I ALWAYS BRAG ABOUT is our crackerjack team of young *flower* girls and how things run smooth as silk thanks to their Gen X, Y, and Z knowledge of new millennium technology, amazing attention to detail, and youthful exuberance.

I, on the other hand, need a drool nap every day around three o'clock and have trouble with the microwave. As vast as the chasm may be between us, there is one great equalizer: cars. We are all girls and, at the risk of offending the more feminist among us, all fairly helpless when faced with auto issues.

It was a brisk, bright February day in Alabama, and we were gearing up for a big floral and fashion event with one of our advertisers. All ducks were in their respective rows, and the team had mobilized to the venue—all except me.

Leaving from home to head to the event, I had forgotten my husband's caveat about the car being low on gas, but the gauge said I had 27 miles till empty. I think it was missing a decimal point, though, because no sooner had I crossed the highway one minute from home than the car began to sputter out. I managed to get off the road but was very glad no young *flower* girls were within earshot as I hurled a few un-flowery words in the general direction of my home and hearth.

When I calmed down, I did what I always do—called my trusty assistant. She came to pick me up, and we abandoned the vehicle on the side of the road.

The event was a triumph in every way. The Los Angeles fashion designer who'd flown in was delighted at the success of the show, as were our advertisers. The guests were reluctant to leave when the party was over (always a good sign) and ended up lingering on into the afternoon visiting and shopping. We *flower* girls all stood around basking in our glory and then finally acknowledged we had to get back to work. "Let's get back to the office and tweet about our wonderful success!"

Floating along in that roseate glow of a job well done, one of our girls (the one in charge of the event) got into a rear-ender in the parking lot, and poof—the bubble burst, as her shiny new ride sustained a major bruise. Our *flower* girl, of course, kept her cool and was a paragon of grace and poise.

Meanwhile, my trusty assistant and I bought gas, filled up my vehicle, and I was off—or not. The engine still wouldn't turn over. *What do you mean you can't leave your flashers on for seven hours without running down the battery?!?!*

By this time I was ready to roll the car into the woods and leave it. But I did the next best thing. I abandoned it there AGAIN and caught a ride home with T.A.

The next day, as I prepared to commiserate with my fellow victim of car catastrophes, I learned that to boost her spirits, our *flower* girl marched back into the store to treat herself to a little retail therapy. I smiled and thought, *Well hey, I got a shiny, new gas can out of the deal.* I'm always looking for the pony. ❧

Rose Bush's Southern hospitality
is put to the test in:

pet peeve

MANY OF YOU MAY NOT BE AWARE that
flower has finally moved out of the International Headquarters (my guest house) into a
for-real office—which is still a cozy cedar shake
cottage, but larger and just down the road from
the original office behind the Bush residence.

Phew! Now we can really spread out, get
more work done, have everyone in one place,

and be "pet free." (For the newer *flower* reader, our office kitty and English setter had made life a bit difficult and somewhat odiferous on occasion around the "home office.")

Happily ensconced in our new digs, one afternoon I received a call from one of our most distinguished and celebrated *flower* fans. I leaned back leisurely in my new lumbar-supported office chair and began to converse with said bigwig when, all of a sudden, I saw a geyser-like movement out of the corner of my eye.

Without letting on that anything was amiss, I began to sweat profusely and listen to the caller rather half-heartedly as two neighborhood dogs continued to dig up our newly planted perennial bed, conveniently located just outside my window for my viewing pleasure. (The geyser-like movement was fast-moving dirt dug up and out into the newly mown yard.)

I wanted to laugh—or cry. I definitely wanted to beat on the window and stop the carnage, but I knew I was in that most unenviable of all places—utter helplessness. So I turned my full attention back to the still-talking caller. When I finally got off the phone, I ran outside shooing the two agents of destruction off the property and then called the landscaper with my tale of woe.

A few canine-free weeks had passed, and it was the night of *flower*'s party to celebrate the printing of the summer issue. I had planned and decorated the new *flower* house to a fair thee well for her first fête, and the evening was in full swing when I noticed a huddle of *flower* girls outside—leaning over, laughing, and petting something. Curious, I joined the group and promptly realized that the party had been crashed by none other than one of the "diggers."

"Isn't she cute!" exclaimed one *flower* girl.

"Look how she just lets you pet her! She's so sweet," sighed another.

"And she's named after my favorite female vocalist!!" squealed a third, after eyeing her monogrammed collar.

Seething, and ready to haul "Stevie" to the pound—or at least not let her have any more hors d'oeuvres—I suddenly realized, *That dog was just being a dog. Dogs dig in the dirt, just like we do—they just don't let the perennials get in their way.*

What the heck, Stevie can stay. She's put a lot of sweat equity into the place.

"Lights out" proves easier said than
done for Rose Bush in:

wild board

IT SEEMS THE OLDER I GET, the more I'm
bedeviled by technology. What I think happens
is that the rate of my aging is in direct propor-
tion to the warp speed of esoteric and Byzantine

advancements in high-level gadgetry—which would not be a problem, except, in publishing, a girl's gotta keep up.

There are some days when I'm impressed with myself, like when I recently went to the Apple store, bought an iPad, and got home and was able to read *flower* magazine on it. But then, the next day, I took it on a sales trip and forgot how to turn it on. (Yeah, there was no way I was calling the "Genius Bar" with that question.) I eventually figured it out but emerged even more wobbly than ever in this "brave new world."

The next challenge I faced was one of the sort that I would generally term a happy problem. It beset me in a fabulous hunting lodge where my husband and I were grateful houseguests over a Labor Day weekend. We were on a real getaway, enjoying the beauty, tranquility, and storied hospitality of the Eastern Shore.

After our first dazzling day of tours, outdoor activities, and a delectable dinner, we were fairly giddy at the prospect of our cozy bed in the lodge, when we both realized we couldn't work the computer keypad that controlled all the lights in the house. *That's simple—we'll turn 'em all off manually.*

Forty minutes later, climbing into bed, we realized we'd turned off our bedside lamps and couldn't get them back on—which would be no obstacle for some, but I haven't gone to sleep without reading first since before I could read. However, I soldiered on and eventually fell asleep counting my blessings, only to wake up after a few minutes with the distinct feeling of being watched.

I looked up and noticed a can light we'd been unable to douse, which was illuminating a very big, very alive-looking wild boar trophy—his beady black eyes, large snout, and menacing tusks giving this fairly intrepid *flower* girl a bit of a fright. After waking my husband to switch places with me, he harrumphed, "Great, now we're both awake."

The next day was as wonderful as the one before, filled with gorgeous people, places, and parties, but we were met with the same technical difficulties come bedtime. Though we progressed to figuring out how to leave our bedside lamps on for reading, the can light still defiantly shone— all night—on the wild boar.

After our third day, which was a replica of the first two only even more wonderful, as I lay in our cocoon-like bed gazing up at the boar, still brilliantly illuminated by the recalcitrant can light, something in me took over. I was seized with a burning desire and determination to TURN THAT LIGHT OFF.

I crept around, found the keypad, and began to punch every square on the board. Of course, all the lights came on, went off, some stayed on, some extinguished—flood lights, kitchen lights, bedroom chandelier light, porch lights, mudroom lanterns, on and on.

Then suddenly, on the verge of giving up, I found myself in total darkness—total—even the boar was in darkness. I squealed inwardly and jumped back into bed. I lay there for a good long while, reveling in my triumph, eager to show off my newfound "techno skills" for my husband the next night, when I suddenly remembered with sad irony, *Dang it, we're leaving tomorrow.* ❧

CPSIA information can be obtained
at www.ICGtesting.com
Printed in the USA
LVIW010342290412
279427LV00008B